One Month,

Make You a Millionaire in One Year.

You don't need to make drastic decisions. You don't need to rob a bank or do anything illegal to successfully achieve your financial goals. I'm talking about above board choices here. There are numerous ways in which you can achieve millionaire status and grow further. I know what you're thinking, isn't 12 months rather ambitious for someone who isn't even making a couple of hundred dollars? To be honest, it is ambitious, but totally attainable!

This book has real life lessons to comfortably change your habits, strategies and recommendations that will set you apart from the 90% of people who are choosing the status quo of laissez faire attitude by settling for less. To be among the 10% of wealth creators and life changers, you need to do what the 90% aren't willing to do. Take action and learn the emulatable skills, lessons, and habits of highly effective people who have reached and surpassed the million-dollar milestone.

This book is not only aimed at awakening the giant in you with self-discipline tips, but it is practical with huge changes resulting from bite-size tasks that you can decide to do in less than five seconds. From taking a reality check of your benchmark, weighing your options, formulating a plan, sticking to what works for you, and removing distractions, to growth potential from lessons on smart investing, guide to easy side hustles that you can implement on your schedule, you have no choice left but cruise to your millions!

The way I see it, you can choose to remain as you are, or you can read along, commit one month doing one task and stand a chance to change your life forever! It's small actions like buying this book that bring gigantic changes!

SELF-DISCIPLINE AND FOCUS TO BECOME A MILLIONAIRE IN 12 MONTHS

Proven methods of determination, grind, hustle and execution to 10X

Christina Balan

By reading this document, the reader agrees that under no circumstances is the author responsible for any losses, direct or indirect, that are incurred as a result of the use of the information contained within this document, including, but not limited to, errors, omissions, or inaccuracies.

Table of Contents

Introduction

Becoming a millionaire in this era is no longer for the privileged only. You can make a few changes and start seeing massive results! All it takes are minor habit replacements as described within and you will hit that milestone in no time. Although achieving it may seem like a far-fetched idea to the average Joe, with some groundwork it is attainable. You may think that it would take years of labor and lots of start-up capital, and you aren't entirely wrong. However, there is a better and quicker way to achieve this. Before you close this book with the mentality that it is one of those that are promoting get-rich-quick schemes, let me assure you that it is not. See, many of those schemes don't require the core attributes that are entailed in this write-up.

The contents of this book are not only vital to assist you to make your first million, but they come with discipline to see you grow from that level further, and actually have a better relationship with money. The goal is to make millions, keep them, and multiply them. Thus, this book is meant to instill self-discipline that will not only help you get rid of debt, unnecessary purchases, cutting corners, and living beyond your means, but it will also help you to grow from barely making money to operating from an area of abundance.

You will realize that getting rid of and adopting new habits require realization and honesty about your starting point, making a decision to do better, and putting that plan in motion. You cannot only look at millionaires with envy and disdain when they live their best lives when you also have potential to make millions. What makes people bitter and negative about money is because of a number of factors and their belief systems about money. If you grew up around the mentality that money is the root of all evil, or that money doesn't grow on trees, you end up believing that having money is a difficult thing that you're better off without having it in abundance. The real game changer will happen the moment you change your mind set about money (Eker, 2005).

Money is powerful, but you are more powerful if you control its flow in your life, not the other way around. For you to reach a level where you don't stress about money, you need to understand the power you have over it and it will respond to your touch. If you respect money, it will also respect you, and do what it's meant to do, to serve you. If you are honest with your finances, they will honestly serve you. Spending more than what you earn, like most people do, will imprison you into a vicious cycle of bad debt, eating from hand to mouth, and living an unrealistic lifestyle that you will end up hating. Believing that you have the power to attract money, and the potential to grow it, converting that will be a piece of cake.

The importance of this book is to give you a workable solution and options that will drastically change your financial lack to abundance. It will give you a roadmap to riches by guiding you to start with realistic practices, replacing bad habits with great ones, following lessons from successful millionaires, ways to increase your earnings, choosing what works for you, avoiding unnecessary distractions that counteract against your goals. At the end of this book, you will have knowledge of smart investing, great opportunities you can add to your streams of income. You will also know financial mistakes to avoid. I invite you to dive in and cruise to your millions if you believe that your dreams matter!

Chapter 1
Small Actions, Big Changes

So you desire to become a millionaire in 12 months? Grabbing this book is the first action that will yield a great impact towards that goal, so read on. It's no secret that change can be chaotic, disruptive, and uncomfortable. But not all change is like that, only drastic change can be bumpy, that is why I have put that into consideration in this chapter. You don't have to radically transform overnight to see massive results. In fact, when gradually introduced, change is almost unnoticeable until you sit down and do a proper analysis.

Pre-analysis

Before you do anything massive, it is important that you take time to examine your situation. Evaluate your current state of affairs to determine your benchmark. Knowing where you stand with your finances will help you consider what daily habits are working for you and which aren't aligned with your desires and life goals. Taking this time is the first paramount step towards change. Unless you are aware of your choices, you will not do anything but remain constant. That means you are not growing, just aging.

Simple things like your sleeping patterns, eating habits, ways of spending, media you consume, and people you hang around are slowly shaping your life. You've got to be aware of how your life is being impacted daily if you want to look in the mirror and still identify with your reflection. Scrutinize what you do daily, and understand what it means for your current and future status. Simple joys are found in priceless moments. What you're spending time on better be what brings you fulfillment if you don't want to feel drained, and short of energy.

Identify things that are meaningful to you and invest more time doing them. Only then will you eradicate time-wasters and focus on building the life that you desire. It takes less than five seconds to decide to do an activity. Whether it's getting out of bed, hydrating, switching off your phone and picking up a good book, taking a walk or jogging, choosing what to eat, or deciding on how to respond to another person or a situation (Robbins, 2017). Less than five seconds! Use the first month examining these things and being intentional with your five seconds of decision-making.

Plan

What's your plan? What do you have in mind with this goal? What do you need to do that is bringing you closer to making your dream a reality? Do you have to build new connections? Work on your tone, wake up early, read more, or simply be yourself? You have to ensure that your habits and plans are in alignment with your desired goal. Otherwise it's a futile exercise doing things that you cannot use to motivate yourself or be future-focused.

What are you going to do daily towards becoming a better person, a great communicator, a wise decision-maker, a happier, and fulfilled person? A simple smile, a moment to listen, a single page, a glass of water, a mile, or a dollar, is what it takes to change your life. Change is in decisive small actions. Decide today what you need to work on and gradually introduce it to your daily routine.

Chapter 2
Reality Check

People tend to live in a fantasy world with unrealistic expectations. I'm not saying you should not dream of a better life because that would defeat the purpose of this book. You are reading this because you have desires, and are looking for a way to fulfill them. But, let's be honest about a few things that will help determine your next steps to achieving your dreams. Being truthful about your reality is better than complacency of living a façade, and it ignites desire to change your situation, instead of the status quo. A reality check provides a benchmark that you can work from as explained by the factors below.

Age

You are never too old or too young to add a new dream, so age should not be your limitation but your power. Of course, being younger may seem attractive and suggest more opportunities ahead of you and so is the wisdom that comes with adulthood and scars of trial and error. Be honest with your age because it will determine whether you can afford to screw up without care. I don't recommend that you slack because you are young and faced with numerous opportunities at your disposal; if this light bulb hits you in your teens, take advantage of it. Numerous kids have paved a way (Bruce, 2015). And today, we're seeing more and more babies making millions from a few recorded moments of merely being themselves.

If you think that you're now a fossil and don't expect much, think again! Let it be the fuel that propels you to get to the millionaire mark on record time, this book is for you, irrespective of your age. Being young however, means that you can try as many times as possible without losing your energy. And being older means that your time is even more precious, so if you are going to commit to any vehicle towards your dreams, fast cars should be your first preference. This means that you have to be pivotal with your plans, executions, and scaling methods to really understand the financial system that will be discussed in further chapter, because you've got no time to waste.

C.S. Lewis reiterates that you are never too old to reach a goal or to dream a new dream, and I couldn't agree more (quotespedia.org, n.d.). Take a look at the story of *Colonel Sanders*, the pioneer of KFC who reached this milestone at 74 years old, and numerous multimillionaires who made it even after the big 50 (Blufish, 2019). Seriously, your age should not scare you from going after your dreams, instead, being realistic about it should be your driving force to get there and beyond sooner!

Income Bracket

A lot of people tend to ignore this factor and instead of using it to their advantage, they use it to judge themselves as failures in comparison with others on a different path from theirs. Earning peanuts is not a curse. In fact, it has propelled numerous millionaires to beat the odds and come above their situations. The world respects people who are making an impact regardless of their background, but people who rise from nothing seem to be more inspirational than those born with a silver spoon in their mouths.

Be realistic with your income scale, then you will know whether you have to be frugal with your purchases or extravagant. The internet world we live in is a double-edged sword of inspiring many to work hard in order to reach milestones, as well as negatively influencing people to aspire to an unrealistic lifestyle as though it can be achieved without discipline. Just because you see your friends splurging millions for luxuries doesn't mean that you have to forget that you are barely affording basics. Learn to consider your income and be realistic with what lifestyle it can afford you.

Being a low-income earner means you need to be more stringent with what you spend your money on. The same is true for middle-income earners. You have to be true to your level and see it for the inadequacy that it is. This will be a wakeup call from your slumber to look for ways to augment it with other revenues. Take notes from high-income earners, they either have high-income skills or multiple sources of income at their disposal.

Completing a thorough reality check will help you to identify your starting point, what you need to do, and what sacrifices you need to make temporarily in order to reach your goal in 12 months. It's exciting to know that you're determined to put in the work.

Chapter 3
Weigh Your Options

Once you've done a good introspection of where you are, now it's a good time to consider what needs to go and what needs to stay. Looking at your current income stream, can you seriously see it making you a millionaire? How bleak is that millionaire status in a year? Two? Ten? What are you going to do about it? The way I see it, you can either do nothing and forget about being a millionaire in the near future or you can read on and find ways to supplement your income.

Do you need to add a new income-generating skill? Do you have the time to learn it? What adjustments do you need to make to manage your time better in order to fit things that are helping you to gravitate towards that goal? You have to make necessary cuts that are not benefiting you or serving your desired future. If it is social media, unless you are learning how to monetize it, or connecting with your mentors through these platforms, you have no business wasting hours browsing for memes and watching other peoples' lives.

If you are eating out just so that you can check in and snap your meals "for the gram", then maybe it's time to cut going to restaurants for pleasure and look for a side hustle as a food blogger. Paying for a gym membership only to cheat on your exercises? Think about replacing that with free walks, hikes, and rope-skipping from the comfort of your home. A self-disciplined you will be okay with forgoing luxuries for now and investing the money for a delayed gratification. What good does it profit you to overspend on luxuries today only to regret it for all your tomorrows?

Keep only what you can afford! Replace that designer clothing item with a good quality that will last you until you can afford to buy stuff for aesthetics without looking at the price tag. I promise you that if you can temporarily forget about instant gratification, the delayed reward will be worth it and empowering. Make all the necessary cuts and use that money to buy your future.

Chapter 4
Formulate a Plan

Unless you win a lottery or wake up suddenly rich, you cannot afford to be spontaneous with your money and expect to reach your goal overnight. Leave chance-winning to gamblers. Sure you can gamble and strike rich, but without a plan, you will see those riches evaporate just like that. You need a rigid plan to see to your goal.

Visualize It

This is where the people who you are following on social media should serve purpose. Instead of watching those who are at the level of abundance with contempt or using that to self-hate that your life sucks, rather, use that as a source of inspiration. Seeing people who already have what you desire shows that it is possible for you too to achieve it. Drawing a vision board is a necessity here. See yourself achieving your first million dollars. If you must calculate how much you have to make daily, weekly, monthly, or quarterly, do so and remind yourself of this goal daily. Thus, a vision board needs to be where you can visualize it daily.

What will having that million dollars mean to you? What will this breakthrough do for your future? Put your vision board up as a constant reminder of why you need to grind daily to reach it. You need a symbolic gesture for this goal. If you need to write down $1,000,000.00 in 12 months 100 times daily, do it. That gesture will not only send positive intentions to the universe, but it will inspire you to put in some work towards making that dream a reality.

Strategize

No matter how solid a plan looks, if you don't have actions planned to take it off the ground, it will remain as it is, just a plan. To someone who has not attained this milestone, a million dollars in a year can be overwhelming. It may seem like a farfetched and prodigious number that scares you. If you look at it like that, you may even relax and think you've got time to bring this to life. You may procrastinate and leave it to the last impossible moment, and be devastated when it fails.

There is a better way to get more done on schedule. To manage this, break down your action plan into sizable chunks that can be fit in a week, day, or hour. That way, it will be less intimidating and achievable. You will reach it one dollar at a time. Find ways in which you plan for each dollar and where you have to put it to yield your desired return on investment (ROI).

Materialize

See your dollar fetching another dollar for you. In order to witness this, you have to increase your earning potential. A side job or business will see you having an extra income that you may not immediately need to use. Earn an extra dollar, save it, invest it, and see it multiply. Voila! Your plan is now in motion. Make calculations; are they evident to reach the feasibility of your goal? What parameters do you need to adjust? Go ahead and make necessary adjustments, repeat cycles that are working, expand where you need to, and deduce the materialization of your plan as you see yourself nearing fulfillment of your goal.

Chapter 5
Stick to What Works

You don't have to try every proven money-making regimen to reach your goal. Focus on what works for you, the level you're at, your resources, your clientele, and overall factors at your disposal. If you've decided to release a product, let it be what is relevant to your target market.

You are aware that your current revenue needs a boost, right? As you ponder on what you are going to do next, focus on practical ways that are evidently producing desired results. If you're learning a high-income skill, be practical about it, and don't stop until it works for you. If you're selling a product, have a timed target for your sales.

Sticking to what works requires you to step up your game and crunch the numbers. If your day job takes up more of your time but pays you less than your side hustle, it makes no sense why you would choose to stay at it. Be bold and put more effort on what will get to your destiny quicker.

You cannot be comfortable spending half your time building your boss's dreams. If you're too tired to work on your dreams, then maybe they are not that important to you. Your WHY needs to be bigger than your HOW. You will find a way to make it work. If it means depriving yourself of sleep sometimes, you will do it.

Diversify your portfolio only when you can. Learn a skill or invest in an equity at a reasonable time, instead of exhausting yourself or funds trying everything at your disposal. Calculate whether something is lucrative or not before trying something else. If one investment brings great returns, don't be tempted to jump to a new one.

Be practical! You don't have to quit your job without a plan on how to cater for what your salary does. Rather use your salary to finance your dream. If your salary is only enough to take you to work so that you can get paid to come to work, it's clear that it's not working. Be brave and look for something that works.

Chapter 6

Remove Distractions

A goal as large as aspiring to become a millionaire in twelve months surely needs a sacrifice. Sacrifice is not only about depriving yourself of the things you love, but temporarily postponing them to a later period. Choosing to sacrifice your time with friends to be alone to re-energize for an assignment or future tasks will only benefit. Be focused with how you spend your time and refuse to be distracted from your goal.

Along the way of being frugal with your finances, there will be temptations to squander your proposed funds by impulse buying, or by entering into temporary debt; try by all means to avoid shifting your focus from your goal. You may have the urge to instantly satiate your desires by splurging your budget on distractions. This is one of the hardest things to do as it's a battle against your willpower. Be prepared to hear your mind convincing you otherwise, but also be disciplined to overcome temptations. You're halfway through your goal, don't look at how far you still have to go, but commend yourself on how far you've come.

Although social media is a powerful tool, it's important to know when to refrain from it and when to capitalize on it. Unless it is advantageous to be on social media, consider cutting down or limit the time you spend on it. Be disciplined with your access to material things and remove distractions.

Another urge to avoid is withdrawing your current profits midway to channel them elsewhere. The previous chapter clearly suggests that you stick with what works for you. If the plan has worked for you so far, why would you be counterintuitive towards it? Don't be the enemy of your progress. Identify deviations from your original plan and be aware of temptations that pose as opportunities and shun them. If you have managed to reduce your debt, reinvest your money, build a nest, or generally stayed on top of your game so far, you've got every reason to celebrate this milestone. Being half-way means half-done, which is way better than when you started. Don't be distracted by anything or anyone! Remain focused, you're almost there!

Chapter 7
Be Frugal

B e strict with your finances. Be accountable for your actions. Cheating on your financial plan can set you back, so be strict with how you access your saved, invested, budgeted funds. By now I'm assuming that you are a well-disciplined person, but if you are still struggling, consider using strict measures. For instance, make use of stop orders or have an accountable person to assist you to follow through with your plan. Document that you have been faithful with monthly budget cuts, healthy meals instead of UberEats, read more books on finances, and listen to more finance related podcasts.

Remember that nobody sees the process of the actual work, just the results of following a strict mandate until one is celebrated for reaching a milestone. Keep that in mind and aspire to celebrate that victory. Being economical is not easy or comfortable, but it is worth it in the end! When you reach your goal, you will thank yourself for sticking to the plan, and I celebrate you ahead of schedule, because I believe in you to put this information to practice. Be strict with the plan, the amount, the strategy, and don't cheat yourself.

Find creative ways that will help you spend less on your day to day expenses. It is said that if you are being creative, you are probably not consuming, but instead, creating (Badr, 2020). Consider some cool DIY projects before spending money on things. These projects can be shared with family and turn into fun activities done collectively. Take free walks and hikes instead of paid funtimes. Visit a library or find readers to exchange your books with. Consider cleaning and cooking for yourself.

If you have to be thrifty to reach your goal, don't be apologetic about it. Wash your car, split chores with your kids, and make them fun. They may call you a cheapskate, but tomorrow they will ask you for lessons, so be frugal and non-apologetic about what you need to do.

Chapter 8
Smart Investing

Be smart and intentional with how you invest your money. It becomes pointless to be frugal only to babysit your money. Find ways that will maximize your earning potential. There is a reason why rich people don't save money but invest it. Be smart with where and how you invest, starting with learning the rules of the game before playing. Invest in a good education on what you consider as your golden goose, don't just be happy to see golden eggs without knowing the source. Learn and earn. This means that you don't jump into opportunities without doing your due diligence. Invest in what you love and love what you invest in, it is your golden goose afterall.

Passive Income

Make your money work for you, remember we already established what a good servant it can be to you! There are only 24 hours in a day so to avoid exhaustion, find ways to make it work for you without your physical presence. You're spending money even while sleeping, so find lucrative ways to make money in your sleep. Things like affiliate marketing, dropshipping, informational products, and royalties can be earned from nothing and with a solid foundation, once they take off, there is no stopping them to keep giving you money.

If you have good capital, buy a golden goose such as the stock market, yield farming, or crypto staking. With basic information on where to put your money, you can invest it in stocks, farms (not referring to agriculture here), and coins that you get paid for simply holding them, or for being a liquidity provider. Whatever you do, find ways to earn passive income, and you will reach your desired level quicker, especially if you deploy the point below.

Compounding

Compound interest is the eighth wonder of the world. He who understands it earns it...he who doesn't...pays it. —Albert Einstein

Compound Interest entails making money on your investments with interest, and adding that interest to the initial investment to make more interest on it as well. If you are paid in dividends, buy more stock. Re-invest the return of your investment. Don't be quick to embezzle your profits, rather re-invest them (Haotanto, 2016).

Dollar Cost Averaging

Dollar cost averaging (DCA) is an investment strategy that investors use to build wealth over time, to neutralize volatility in the equity market, and thus, one of the smart investing tools (Hayes & Chen, 2021). Whether you are buying stocks, cryptocurrencies, or whichever avenue you are putting your money into, you will reach the millionaire milestone quicker when you buy or invest equal parts at intervals. Some days you will buy at high price points, and others at relatively lower prices. On average, you will have bought more of that asset, which will in turn make you more money.

Think Long-Term and Start Early

By now, you must be keen to start working towards your goal. Don't procrastinate, but do it while you are still zealous. The best way is to start early, so don't slumber on this information without taking any action! Millionaires don't stop at their first million, they think long term. Play the long game, and you will see your turnaround. Being a smart investor means spotting opportunities early and delaying to reap the benefits.

Chapter 9

12 Easy Hustles You Can Start Today To Boost Your Income

F or an avenue to qualify as easy, practical, and overall beneficial, it must be able to assist you in supplementing your main income, with the potential to generate more, given the time and scaling room. Robert Farrington eloquently details that the best side hustles are those that have flexible scheduling, earning, and growth potential (Farrington, 2019).

Here are some of the best hustles that fit these criteria:

1. Blogging

2. Freelancing

3. Tutoring

4. Food delivery

5. Car renting

6. House listing (Airbnb)

7. Buying and reselling stuff (flipping on eBay, Etsy, NFT marketplaces, etc.)

8. Moving furniture

9. Becoming a handyman

10. Online surveys

11. Being a promoter (influencer)

12. Create a digital product (e-course, ebook, masterclass, etc.)

Chapter 10

12 Lessons from Millionaires

Success leaves clues. —Tony Robbins

L earn these lessons, model the methods, and celebrate yourself when you finally experience the results of attaining your goals. Amongst many habits and characters, wealthy people possess the following traits that you can learn:

1. Goal setting and planning (vision boards)

2. Communication (constant emails, calls, mixers, and face-to-face interaction)

3. Networking (always making new contacts, increasing their net-worth by the company they keep)

4. Punctual (they start their days early and respect time)

5. Sales

6. Voracious readers and critical thinkers

7. Exercising and sticking to routines

8. Well-organized

9. Money management

10. Philanthropic

11. Problem solving

12. Branding (responsible brands) (Badziag, 2019)

Chapter 11

Common Financial Mistakes to Avoid

A s much as this book is mainly motivational, it is paramount that we include some of the limiting factors to attain your dreams in record time. There are costly mistakes that you may stumble upon if you are not careful.

Frivolous Spending

Just because you start seeing little profits doesn't give you a license to be extravagant with your spending. You are not yet there, so focus on maintaining your level and growing it, until you reach the next level described in the next chapter. Just as it took one dollar to start building wealth, losing a great fortune also happens one dollar at a time (Norris, 2021).

Get it Now, Pay Later

It's easy to spend the money you don't have, getting items you need on credit, and paying for them later. However, it's a quick way to enslave yourself to debts. Find ways to quickly settle your debts, pay-off your credit cards, and stop living on borrowed money!

Prioritizing Liabilities Over Assets

Don't be tempted to buy items that cost you money, instead, go for income generating assets. Unless you're using your smartphone for content creation or working on featured apps, there is no need to upgrade to the latest model. Note that what are known as assets, can be liabilities if they cost you for keeping them, and what are known as liabilities can take the form of assets if having them generates income for you. Prioritize items that appreciate in value.

Not Having Emergency Funds

With many people comfortable living paycheck to paycheck, it has become a norm for them not to have any floating fund that is allocated for those unpleasant and unplanned emergencies. Not having these insurance, hospital, and disaster relief funds, will either cause you to dip your hands into the honeypot which is eating away your future, or to go back to the vicious cycle of debts. Be responsible with your funds and always keep some in the easy access account for when it starts to drizzle!

Not Having a Plan

This is equal to lack of ambition. You can't just live any way you want irrespective of your finances. Have a plan in motion and you will see that a structured life has order while a planless life is chaotic.

Not Tracking Your Finances

You need to be intentional and strict in tracking the movements of your money, whether it's towards or away from you all the time. This will determine your relationship with money. Track it and analyze the flow of money in your life. Be worried if most of the time money is deserting you and leaving you stranded, and aspire to have it being frequently attracted to you.

Not Paying Yourself First

From every income you get, pay yourself first, you're the one who works hard after all. The Rich Dad has been preaching this since 1997, yet many still don't get this concept and are far from practicing it (Kiyosaki & Letcher, 1997). Don't be one of them! Prioritize your long-term financial well-being before you spend any fraction of your salary or income. Let deductions for bills and other things come after you've secured your future.

Procrastinating

Reading this book and putting it aside for weeks—even days—without taking any action will likely make you forget this information. When you get new opportunities to grow your money, don't take too much time sleeping on them, some opportunities love fast action-takers because success loves speed (Ringer, 2014)!

Get Rich Quick Schemes

It's easy to build consistency with managing your risks and developing a habit of patience. But greed can make your accumulated wealth go up in smoke in no time through so-called get-rich-quick schemes. Don't fall victim to phishing sites or fall prey to fly-by-night platforms that promise you heaven-on-earth in such a quick period. True returns take time, don't let your impatience lose your accumulated fortune. following the road map to success

Chapter 12

Making Millions on Autopilot

I'm not sure about you but the ultimate goal is to be on this level! I get the necessary steps that were deployed previously, they were a mere starting point to get you out of a frustrating financial level to wealth accumulation. However, true and abundant wealth is made on autopilot! Strive to work smart until your investments afford you the level where your millions go out to work and fetch their brothers and sisters while you sip on champagne in your private jet or mojitos on your luxury yacht.

Can you picture yourself on this level? If you followed every tip from those who made it, as detailed in the previous chapters, then you will have arrived at your goal. This is where your self-discipline, focus, hustle, grind, and sacrifices finally pay off! This is where you scale your wealth through automated methods, leverage on social media, technology, quality staff, and resources! I wish you all the best as you work towards this next level! Level up, and cruise to your millions because that's the level that you deserve and should be attaining!

Conclusion

Congratulations on reading up to this point! With the rich content you've just consumed, I have no doubt that you're full of value and ready to execute. Becoming a millionaire needs not remain a desire, but an attainable goal on schedule. Not only did this book show the practicality and proof that with self-discipline, hustle, and grind, you can achieve more, but it also provided easy to model tools and options to set this plan in motion. I wish you all the success in your journey to living your truth as a millionaire!

References

Ally, D. (2016, March 8). The 12 skills I learned from millionaires. Business Insider. https://www.businessinsider.com/the-12-skills-that-helped-me-become-a-millionaire-at-age-24-2016-3?IR=T#-4

AZ Business Magazine. (2019, July 9). Here are 10 people who struck it rich after 50. AZ Big Media. https://azbigmedia.com/business/economy/here-are-10-people-who-struck-it-rich-after-50/

Badr. (2020, July 1). 7 Ways To Be Frugal And Save Money. Make Money for Sure. https://www.makemoneyforsure.com/ways-to-be-frugal-and-save-money/

Badziag, R. (2019, June 21). I interviewed 21 self-made billionaires about their secrets to wealth and success—here's what I learned. CNBC. https://www.cnbc.com/2019/06/21/self-made-billionaires-the-6-habits-of-massive-wealth-and-success.html

Bruce, K. (2015, January 23). Wanna Be A Millionaire? Learn From These 12 Kids Who Already Are. Lifehack. https://www.lifehack.org/articles/money/wanna-millionaire-learn-from-these-12-kids-who-already-are.html

Eker, T. H. (2005). Secrets of the millionaire mind : mastering the inner game of wealth. Collins, An Imprint Of Harpercollins

Publishers Ltd. https://www.amazon.com/Secrets-of-Millionaire-Mind-audiobook/dp/B01F7O1FKW/ref=sr_1_1?crid=18M2UFOXO VLF7&keywords=secrets+of+the+millionaire+mind&qid=164 1511454&sprefix=secrets+of+the+%2Caps%2C1311&sr=8-1

Elkins, K. (2016, February 16). 19 things keeping you from getting rich, according to a journalist who spent his career studying millionaires. The Independent. https://www.independent.co.uk/news/business/19-things-stopping-you-from-getting-rich-a6877251.html

Farrington, R. (2019, May 24). 15 Best Side Hustles You Can Start Earning With Now. The College Investor. https://thecollegeinvestor.com/23078/best-side-hustles/

Financial Wolves. (2021, April 5). 10 Ways You Can Make Money While You Sleep. Financialwolves.com. https://financialwolves.com/make-money-while-you-sleep/

Ganatra, M. (2021, August 3). What Is Smart Investing? 10 Ways To Do It. Forbes Advisor INDIA. https://www.forbes.com/advisor/in/investing/what-is-smart-investing-10-ways-to-do-it/

Haotanto, A. V. (2016, January 23). Compounding: The Eight Wonder Of The World. The New Savvy. https://thenewsavvy.com/plan/savings/the-eight-wonder-of-the-world-compounding/

Hayes, A., & Chen, J. (2021, August 19). Dollar-Cost Averaging (DCA) Definition. Investopedia.

https://www.investopedia.com/terms/d/dollarcostaveraging.asp

Kiyosaki, R. T., & Lechter, S. L. (2002). Rich dad, poor dad : what the rich teach their kids about money-- that the poor and middle class do not! Sphere.

Newlands, M. (2014, October 6). 20 easy steps to become a millionaire. Business Insider. https://www.businessinsider.com/easy-ways-to-become-a-millionaire-2014-10?IR=T

Norris, E. (2021, July). Top 10 Most Common Financial Mistakes. Investopedia. https://www.investopedia.com/personal-finance/most-common-financial-mistakes/

quotespedia.org. (n.d.). You are never too old to set another goal or to dream a new dream. - C.S. Lewis - Quotespedia.org. Www.quotespedia.org. Retrieved January 6, 2022, from https://www.quotespedia.org/authors/c/c-s-lewis/you-are-never-too-old-to-set-another-goal-or-to-dream-a-new-dream-c-s-lewis/

Ringer, R. (2014, May 20). Success Loves Speed - by Robert Ringer. RobertRinger.com. https://robertringer.com/success-loves-speed/

Robbins, M. (2017). The 5 second rule : transform your life, work, and confidence with everyday courage. Savio Republic.

Robbins, T. (2016). Modeling Psychology: Definition, Examples & More | TonyRobbins. Tonyrobbins.com. https://www.tonyrobbins.com/stories/unleash-the-power/the-key-to-success-model-the-best/#:~:text=As%20Tony%20Robbins%20says%2C%20%E2%80%9CSuccess

Slide, C. (2021, September 14). How to Become a Millionaire. Money Crashers. https://www.moneycrashers.com/how-to-become-millionaire/

TopThink. (2019, August 10). 12 Tips to Build Unbreakable Self-Discipline. Www.youtube.com. https://www.youtube.com/watch?v=1smrJfW3FE8

Made in the USA
Columbia, SC
27 June 2022

62350115R00026